D1709070

Journey with the
Whitetail

JOURNEY WITH THE WHITETAIL

A Photographic Exploration Through Field & Forest by Mark Raycroft

WILLOW CREEK PRESS

Published by Willow Creek Press, Inc.
P.O. Box 147, Minocqua, Wisconsin 54548

Printed in China

ACKNOWLEDGEMENTS

This journey has been nothing short of amazing and there are many people to whom I wish to extend a heartfelt thank you!

First, to the love of my life, my wife Pili, thank you for always sharing my vision and for being my strongest supporter over the past 20 years!

Next, to my wonderful children, Martha and Andrew, thank you for encouraging me on my many adventures!

To my parents for introducing me to the wonders of the wilderness and for always cheering me on!

To my many friends who have shared in these adventures, I am grateful for your time, generosity, and humor: Dolf DeJong, Bill Gadzos, Bob and Alma Avery, Brad Dake, Darla Outhout, Brenda Brookes, Darren Raycroft, Jeff Raycroft, Jason Griffiths, Luke Vander Vennen, Ted Hill, and Joshua Hambleton.

To Chris Mutton, thank you for your friendship and for your video editing expertise.

And a special thank you to the ambitious and talented team at Willow Creek Press: Donnie Rubo, Tom Petrie, Jeremy Petrie, Sara Olson and Amy Kolberg.

I dedicate this book to my Dad. Thank you for sharing your love of the woods and for always encouraging me to follow my dreams.

Introduction

After decades of photographing North American wildlife, White-tailed deer remain the enduring and fascinating focus of my career. Their incredibly acute senses, explosive agility, rugged hardiness and complex behavioral patterns make them one of the most interesting and challenging animals to photograph.

My passion for these elusive animals began at a young age when my Dad took me on my first hunting adventure. Countless hours surrounded by wilderness convinced me that these experiences make me feel whole. I continued further into the world of wildlife and whitetails by studying wildlife biology at University. After receiving my degree, I began my career as a wildlife photographer and author in earnest. In travelling to the edges of the continent, and to many awe-inspiring destinations in between, by autumn my lens always focuses back to whitetails!

I hope that as you turn the pages of this book you'll feel immersed in the journey of the whitetail. This photographic voyage begins with summer, the season of growth and nourishment, then transforms as autumn's colors and frosts provide a backdrop for the elaborate behaviors that exemplify the whitetail rut, and then, see how deer adapt to face the challenges of winter.

After you've enjoyed these pages, I invite you to place the accompanying disc into your DVD player, sit back, and allow the 36-minute film to guide you through field and forest as we follow the whitetail through these seasons. May this visual journey deepen your understanding and appreciation of this icon of the wilderness.

Mark Raycroft

SUMMER

Deer are an ever-present link to the natural wonders that surround us. We admire their incredible senses, superior agility, and crowning antlers.

Dawn's yellow glow shines upon a majestic buck as he pauses during his early morning travels.

This whitetail's summer coat is luminous in the richness of first light.

No taller than the blades of grass that surround it, this tiny newborn fawn quietly moves to a new bed. A fawn's white spots mimic the dappled shadows of light broken by a forest canopy or lush pasture.

Weighing only six pounds at birth, newborn fawns can stand within minutes, but lack the strength and agility to outrun predators during the first few weeks of life.

An impressive black bear prowls the north woods, his keen nose searching for food. Spring grasses are his primary diet, but a whitetail fawn would be a welcomed appetizer. With the black bear mating season occurring through late spring, this boar will spend a lot of calories searching out and competing for mates.

A doe and her fawn stay in close contact throughout the first year of its life. A mother recognizes her young by sight, sound, and smell.

Safety in numbers applies only until the rut. For 11 months of the year bucks often buddy-up with similarly aged individuals. During summer a deer's home range is about one square mile.

Males and females usually occupy different home ranges in summer, the does inhabiting the areas with the premium forage. The only time the two sexes overlap is when they share a lush food source.

To escape from swarms of biting flies, bucks frequently bed in open areas during the summer, taking advantage of the slightest breeze. Their blood-engorged growing antlers are particularly sensitive.

Their size making them more vulnerable to predators, fawns must always be alert and ready to bolt for cover. With ears like mini radar this spritely fellow isn't likely to miss much.

Antlers are visible evidence of a buck's age, health,and genetic advantage. They have been coveted and respected by humans for millennia. This fraternal group of bucks sport impressive racks.

Areas that are rich in summer forage and also provide adequate cover area are a haven for whitetails.

Subtle scents that are imperceptible to humans are essential to the daily communications of the whitetail. Glands, pheromones, and tiny molecules carrying pertinent information constantly play a role in how this relatively quiet species responds to the world around them.

For many people, the glimpse of a deer creates an immediate link with our wild spirit. We remain motionless, marveling at a sight that is gone too soon.

Humans have transformed the landscape throughout much of the whitetail's range. Deer are often the benefactor. This lush field of soybeans is a welcome breakfast for this mature doe.

Summer is a season of plenty for the northern species. Like humans, whitetails feast on the bounty of the harvest. Maximizing growth for the trials that lay ahead is critical for mature bucks. They'll soon face the intense physical demands of the rut, closely followed by the scarcity of winter.

A late-summer field provides nourishing forage. Mature bucks prefer to feed in smaller, more secretive openings, to stay within a few bounds of forest cover.

Nature's daily rhythm does not have a clock. It is guided by day length, sustenance, and survival.

As summer winds down, the days shorten and buck's testosterone levels begin to rise. As antlers finally harden into bone, bucks impatiently put them to use. With a still tender rack, this buck mock-rubs a moth mullein plant, which is sure to be replaced with trees in the weeks ahead.

Although every set of antlers is unique, the multiple brow tines on this mature buck are rare. This coming autumn, his combatants won't appreciate his added hardware when sparring begins. The sticker points will surely elevate him in the dominance hierarchy.

Foretelling the action to come, this mature buck wishfully tests a nearby doe's readiness to breed even though it's only August.

Seasonal shift: the end of summer is marked by a buck's bloody rack. His antlers now solid bone, the once nourishing velvet is rubbed off to reveal his crowning glory. This is a painless twenty-four hour process.

AUTUMN

The spotted coat of youth is replaced in early September with a mantle of brown. The fawn now looks like a miniature version of his mother. The majority of his diet is now vegetation but he will nurse on occasion.

Swiftness coupled with sharp senses has enabled the whitetail to thrive throughout much of North America.

The redness of this 10-pointer's rack indicates that he has recently stripped off his summer velvet. Rain, dew, and a buck's imperative to rub, will quickly fade the crimson from the bone.

Wisely cautious, a mature buck remains within the shadows of the forest during his dawn travels. Game trails, some new, some decades old, meander through field and forest, following the path of least resistance, while concealing the movements of deer young and old.

With his antlers now ready for battle, this prime-aged buck's testosterone levels are spiking, resulting in increased mating behavior. He's in peak condition with his neck beginning to swell up and strengthen for the clashes that characterize the rut.

The mists of dawn surround a mature 10-pointer as he feeds along a field edge before returning to a secretive day-bed. September is a time to focus on feeding and weight gain.

A true marvel of the whitetail species, this northern buck exemplifies good nutrition and superior genetics. For many hunters this would be the buck of a lifetime!

Skirting the forest edge, a heavy-beamed buck feeds on freshly fallen acorns. These protein-rich nuts help deer to bulk up for the rut.

Acorn fact: White oaks produce acorns every year, while Red oaks only produce their nut mast every other year.

Where soybean meets corn a deer's trough overflows.

Come October, a field of soybeans will become a routine feeding destination for local deer.

The deciduous forests of North America undergo an awe-inspiring transformation each autumn, one of the true marvels of this great planet.

Antlers are the architecture of genetics. The more elaborate the architecture the more likely the survival of the genes.

His forest home transformed into a marquee of gold, this buck trolls for freshly fallen acorns and beech nuts, favorite foods of autumn.

A testosterone-charged buck creates a licking branch, a scent-laden signpost, which serves to introduce him to nearby females, while warning potential rivals that he's in the area.

The pines whisper stories as the wind filters through their needles; stories that the deer know all too well, of times old when the girth of a tree could shield him and the song of wolves filled the night.

The October pre-rut is still a time of feeding and rest, necessary to conserve energy for the relentless mating season. Once the first doe comes into heat, bucks will begin their search for mates and will continue undeterred for three solid weeks!

Evidence of a mood swing! With more and more fresh rubs appearing on trees, it's clear that the males are gearing up for the rut and are creating plenty of signage to stake out their territory.

Speed, grace and muscle, whitetails are resilient, adaptable survivors.

It's amazing how a heavy-antlered buck can sprint across a field and not slow down when he leaps into and through the forest. A buck perfectly understands the dimensions of his antlers, twisting and turning his head adeptly while in full flight, so as to never get caught up on a tree or branch!

Crunch! The buck's head snaps to full attention! His ears, eyes and nose work in unison to reveal the source of the sound. If it is another deer he'll resume his morning routine. If it is a coyote or wolf, he'll explode from the opening and within a few bounds disappear into the forest.

A hidden stream quenches the thirst of a sly buck.

Bucks that share the same home range will joust numerous times through early to mid-autumn. This ritual sparring refines their fighting technique for when everything is on the line.

Females flee to briefly test the fitness of a new suitor.
This awe-inspiring buck is up to the challenge!

A healthy whitetail doe pauses along the edge of a soybean field. In the weeks ahead she'll draw the attention of every buck within miles.

The visual essence of the rut: a mature buck lip curls while on a doe's trail to test whether or not she's in heat and will be receptive to his advances. If she is, he'll continue tracking along her scent trail. If she's not, he'll search for a different doe.

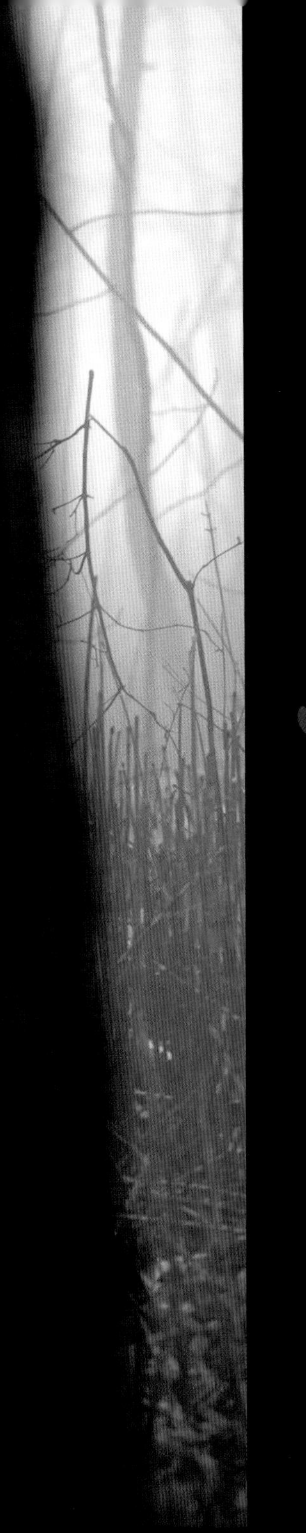

Phantoms of the forest, some mature bucks are nocturnal, only leaving the shelter of the forest under the veil of darkness.

The sound of bone clashing against bone echoes through the hardwoods as two mature bucks spar to test one another's strength before the fast approaching rut.

Wilderness is the scent of the forest, the whisper of the breeze, and the sight of something wild.

An active scrape is the scent-laden, primary communication hub of the whitetail rut. Bucks paw bare the earth below a licking branch, then urinate over their musky tarsal glands, leaving a clear calling card to receptive does.

Making his way along a hardwood ridge, this buck heads to a grove of nearby oaks. When acorns and beech nuts are available, bucks prefer them over foods such as farmed crops, because they can feed during the daylight

Stomp! A mature doe senses something is amiss as sh enters a soybean field during her evening feeding routine Deer stomp their front hoof in an effort to convinc the perceived threat to expose itself. If it does, they'r

For whitetails, every breeze carries information relevant to their survival. The threat of predators, the scent of food, water or the lure of the opposite sex, can all be conveyed on the slightest air current.

Vying for top position in the dominance hierarchy is an annual tradition for mature bucks. Antler size and shape, body mass and fighting technique all factor into a buck's reproductive success.

Comrades no longer, friendly sparring matches become a thing of the past as soon as the first doe enters estrous—all deals are off!

A hunter's dream... a mature 11-pointer in full rut emerges in an autumn clearing. A sighting like this is worth every bit of effort of rolling out of bed during the pre-dawn darkness to be afield at daybreak.

Bucks carve the outer bark from trees by using the gnarly base of their antlers. Mature bucks will rub theirs antler bases smooth by the end of autumn!

With his body at its annual peak, muscles ready, neck swollen and antlers polished, this prime-aged buck eagerly faces the challenges of the rut.

Flanked by glowing autumn leaves, a mature buck protectively watches over the doe that he is tending.

Fiery hues of autumn foliage backdrop the annual deer rut. This lustful male has caught the scent of romance. Flehmen, more commonly referred to as lip curling, is how a male uses a small organ in his upper oral region to test if the female that he's pursuing is actually in heat.

An imposing buck makes quick work rubbing the bark from a small sapling. Shards of the tree cling to his antlers. Not only does he leave his scent on this territorial signpost, he also creates a visual cue warning all other bucks that they're on his turf!

Hair bristling and ears flattened, a buck is agitated by the sight of a challenger. A stiff-legged, quartering walk is the final warning offered to the other male.

thick forest provides shelter for the wise, wary
hitetail.

Under a full moon at twilight; whitetails are sure to be on the move. Some deer experts call this "The Hunter's Moon," as it's believed that the second full moon following the autumnal equinox marks the

The rising sun greets a rut-crazed dominant buck as he lip curls while hot on the trail of a doe.

The aroma of a doe in heat is nature's most intoxicating fragrance to a rutting buck.

A dominant buck works a licking branc
hardwood ridge.

Watching over a doe in heat, a mature buck is always ready to confront challengers to battle for the right to reproduce.

The tending buck will remain with an estrous doe for about 48 hours, or for as long as she's in heat. Once her heat cycle is over he'll quickly move on, frantically searching for the scent of his next mate.

A prime-aged rutting buck, glances back whi
tracking a doe scent trail across a field. During th
rut a buck's range may increase to 5 miles or more.

Through much of November, does are in heat and the rut is in full swing! The scent trail of an estrous doe transfixes a noble buck, luring him from the protection of the forest during midday.

A true anomaly in the whitetail world, caused by a hormonal imbalance, a doe with an overabundance of testosterone sprouts an antler. It will likely remain velvet-covered.

Acutely evolved senses equal survival for the wary whitetail. With a nose that's 1,000+ times superior to a human's, this majestic buck sniffs something on the breeze.

A tending pair will mate many times over a two day period.

Time is a commodity that whitetails don't measure. There's no rush or reason to risk being seen if they sense something is amiss. They freeze on the spot and wait for their superior senses to confirm the source before moving an inch. 10 seconds or 10 minutes make no difference to the whitetail. They're the epitome of patience, survival is paramount. This rule is broken only for the rut.

How many times have we unknowingly passed by wild creatures when walking in the woods? I wish that I knew the answer…

Mother knows best. A wary fawn flustered by a strange scent or sound seeks the matriarch's guidance.

WINTER

The first snowfall warns of changing seasons. It may melt quickly this time, but eventually it will stay, covering preferred food sources and if deep enough, even impede movement.

Contests for the right to breed persist after the first snow arrives in the north country. Bucks continue to spar until the connection between their antlers and skull begins to weaken.

Even on the frigid days of early winter bucks will eagerly check nearby females, hoping to find one more mate.

With snows not yet deep enough to force deer into winter yards, this prime-aged buck trots easily across a frozen field. Perhaps the scent of a wolf caused him to evacuate one bush lot in favor of another?

Deer activity intensifies before a winter storm. Whitetails can sense the sharp drop in barometric pressure and predict that inclement weather is imminent. The hours prior to the storm are spent feeding to prepare for an extended bedding period.

If a doe is not successfully bred during her first heat in November, she will cycle again into estrous 28 days later. It is also believed that about 40% of female fawns may become fertile during their first December.

Deer will eat snow to stay hydrated during winter, but an open stream is preferred if it's close to their wintering yard.

As December progresses, the hope of finding another receptive doe fades and bucks that were bitter rivals only weeks before, again tolerate one another's company to reunite in a "bachelor group." They face the season of nature's greatest challenge together. The extra eyes and ears help to sense lurking predators.

As snow deepens, deer must adjust their feeding habits to adapt, switching from fallen nuts and leaves to cedar, hemlock and woody browse that is above the snowline. This buck has clearly been trying his best to root out any remaining acorns beneath the snow.

Standing stalks of corn that were missed along a field edge become even more of a magnet as snow covers the ground. The corn won't last long with hungry whitetails around.

A doe feeds on browse not yet covered with snow. If winter's trials become too harsh, an impregnated doe can reabsorb one or more of her developing fetuses to conserve energy and focus on her own survival.

Whitetails share their home with many species. On a cold winter's afternoon, a flock of wild turkeys race ahead of a yearling buck to scavenge the final remnants of a cornfield.

Whitetail mothers guide their offspring through the first year of life. After their first birthday, yearling males relocate to new home ranges to disperse the gene pool, while females typically rejoin their mother following the doe's next fawning. These matriarchal groups are lead by the oldest female.

The warming sun is welcomed on a subzero morning, even if the mercury only climbs a few degrees.

As snow depths increase, deer migrate to wintering "yards," congregating where shelter and winter forage can be found. Large groves of evergreens, such as white cedar, can effectively block out the wind and reduce snow accumulation, creating an appealing microenvironment for the local deer herd.

A doe rises to full attention, tail flared, her fawn also aware of danger. It will be a mere second or two before they exit the scene.

Typically, deer won't run if something suspicious only triggers one of their three primary senses. But as soon as the threat is confirmed by a second sense, they will bolt!

Startled by the sight of the coyote, a group of does flee into a forest of thick evergreens.

His agility not hampered by his 200 pound frame, a mature buck launches toward the security of the snowy woods after sensing a threat.

A predator could be around any corner, lurking behind any tree. This constant possibility continues to hone the keen senses of the whitetail.

Whitetails have their sharp senses and are fleet of hoof, but the predators lurking in the north woods are cunning.

Wolves have highly evolved, pack-orientated hunting strategies for pursuing whitetails. Even with these proven tactics their attempts fail more often than they succeed.

Even the biggest bucks can vanish quickly if danger is near. Peering around a tree, something has caught this buck's attention. Was it a wolf's paw crunching on the snow or just a snow-laden twig falling to the forest floor? The next few seconds will reveal the answer.

With the depths of winter approaching, it's time for deer to conserve energy, protect the fat they've collected, and slow their metabolism to survive this harsh season of frozen snowpack and less-nourishing browse.

With a hide made up of insular hollow hairs, this buck's winter coat is so efficient at trapping his body heat that the snow falling onto his back doesn't melt! The ability to stay warm is critical for survival in the northern part of the whitetail's range where temperatures can drop to a frigid -30 at night!

Rising after being bedded through much of the storm, the buck shakes the accumulated snow from his back.

A tree grows rings that can reveal its age, where a buck's antlers do not, as they're shed and re-grown every year. There's no scientific way to accurately guess a buck's age based on his rack. However, the overall size and mass of the bone can help a trained eye to estimate the maturity of their bearer. This mature buck is at least 4 years old.

Whitetail bucks usually shed both antlers within 24 hours. Sometimes they're relieved of both sides within minutes, other times it's two to three days before the second antler is cast off.

A sharp drop in testosterone levels will cause bucks to drop their hefty headgear. Shedding several pounds from their heads helps to conserve energy during the arduous months ahead.

With his antlers recently shed, a mature buck admires the crown still being carried by another male. Northern bucks can drop their antlers as early as mid-December, or keep them through to the end of February. The typical timeframe for antler shedding is from mid-January through to mid-February.